4000 Years
OF Christmas

4000 Years
OF Christmas

A Gift from the Ages

EARL W. COUNT, PH.D.
ALICE LAWSON COUNT

INTRODUCTION
Dan Wakefield

Seastone

BERKELEY, CALIFORNIA

Published by:
Seastone, an imprint of Ulysses Press
P.O. Box 3440
Berkeley, CA 94703-3440
www.ulyssespress.com

The Library of Congress has cataloged the hardback as follows:

Library of Congress Cataloging-in-Publication Data
Count, Earl W. (Earl Wendel), 1899–1996
4000 years of Christmas / Earl Count and Alice Lawson Count :
introduction, Dan Wakefield
p. cm.
Includes bibliographical references and index.
ISBN 1-56975-087-4 (hardcover)
I. Christmas—History.   I. Count, Alice Lawson.   II. Title.
GT4985.C65   1997
394.2663—dc21

ISBN 1-56975-235-4 (paperback)

Printed in Canada by Transcontinental Printing

10 9 8 7 6 5 4 3 2 1

Distributed in the United States by Publishers Group West, in Canada by Raincoast
Books, and in Great Britain and Europe by Airlift Book Company.

TO YOU
WHO HAVE LOVED CHRISTMAS
AND HAVE MADE IT BEAUTIFUL

CONTENTS

INTRODUCTION
by Dan Wakefield

I REMEMBER MY FATHER playing the small foot-pedal organ in the living room of our house in Indianapolis as my mother and I stand beside him singing "O Little Town of Bethlehem." I am seven years old and I know this song and this holiday season are sacred. I feel a quiet thrill as I sing of the everlasting light that "in the dark streets shineth," just as the light from a streetlamp down the block casts a glow through the frosted windowpanes and red, green, blue, white, and yellow lights shine from the evergreen boughs of the tree in the corner. Like millions of people before and since, I absorb the joy and the solemnity of Yuletide, when "the hopes and fears of all the years" are met on Christmas Eve. Life without it would have seemed unthinkable to me, the year routine and ordinary.

I knew as a child that Christmas was a celebration of something new coming into the world with the babe in the manger. I also knew it was accompanied by a whole panorama of song, feast, light, Santa Claus, and presents. I had no idea, though, that so many of the traditions and customs I loved—the "twelve days" of Christmas, bright fires of candle flame and lights on the tree, processions of singing from house to house, feasting and giving of gifts—had roots in a festival of renewal in ancient Mesopotamia two thousand years before Christ was born.

As a child I believed Santa Claus (or "Saint Nick," which I thought was his name in England) was real because I saw him every year at Sears Roebuck and told him what I wanted. I helped my mother set out a "midnight supper" for him on Christmas Eve (coincidentally consisting of my father's favorite snacks when he came home from the late shift at his pharmacy), and lo and behold, the next morning the snacks were eaten and my presents were under the tree, "proof" that Saint Nicholas really was there.

That's all I needed or cared to know about the subject then. Now I'm fascinated to learn that the real Saint Nicholas was the son of well-to-do Christians who lived in a province of Asia Minor in the third century, and who became archbishop of the seaport town of Myra. He inherited his family's fortune, and went to great pains to help people without letting them know he was the benefactor, "slipping gifts into the home of worthy people at night."

I had no idea how varied, rich, and ancient our heritage of Christmas was until I read this gem of a book. Nor did I imagine that familiar practices performed in the small frame house where I grew up in the 1940s also had origins in Babylonian festivals and Roman revels! The survival of customs from such diverse times and cultures throughout history seem to me to a powerful testament to the universality of the human experience. It suggests that we are not only brothers and sisters under the skin, but also in time and space.

Two thousand years before Christ, in the land where the Tigris and Euphrates meet, people felt the weight of the old year as it drew to a close, and needed a sense of renewal to face the new one, just as we do today. "As the old year died, the rules of ordinary living were relaxed" in the households of Mesopotamia, just as they were on Winthrop Avenue in Indianapolis when I was a boy. Then fathers came home early from work, mothers made splendid feasts, and children sang carols from house to house, where windows were lit with electric candles and colored lights on trees twinkled like jewels.

"The rules of ordinary living were relaxed" to such an extent in our house that when relatives came to visit the week before Christmas, the men surreptitiously gathered in the kitchen where my father would draw a pint of bourbon from its hiding place in the broom closet and pass it around to each one for a nip and a sigh of satisfied warmth. That must have been our mild Hoosier version of the Romans' "Saturnalia," the pagan revels of excess that marked that time of the year.

Like those Romans, we also decorated with green boughs to remind us of life's continuance, and lit lamps and candles as they did against the dark. I loved to stare into candle flames or the fire log that had a special meaning at Yuletide. I'm sure the children of faraway lands and times felt much the same awe in centuries and empires past when their minds and imagination were captured by the mystery and meaning of light.

The wish to bring light to the dark, give hope of spring in the dead of winter, and a chance to renew ourselves for another year are universal human desires. Lighting the candles for Hanukkah every December symbolizes such longing in the Jewish faith. The celebration of the birth of Christ by Christians throughout the world, has blended with symbols and customs of thanks and renewal from cultures throughout history and across all borders. The richness of the story of *4000 Years of Christmas* gives new meaning and pleasure to the holiday, and is itself a bountiful gift.

PROLOGUE

❧

THIS IS ONE OF the world's greatest stories. We do not know its beginning, and it has not yet ended. Much of the story is not known—for instance, we do not really know when the Christ Child it venerates was born; or the time and place when Christmas was first celebrated; or exactly how it was that, over the centuries, a bishop-saint of Asia Minor and a pagan god of the Germans merged to become Santa Claus.

Although the Christmas story centers in the Christ Child of Bethlehem, it begins so long before his coming that we find its hero arriving on the scene after more than half of the time of the story has gone by.

Christmas is one of humankind's great experiences. For more than four thousand years, spreading over the earth, it has drawn the loyalties and longings of millions of people, growing always richer as humankind has matured.

To what, then, shall we liken Christmas? It is like a seed that is planted within the soil. It springs  upward and downward. Upward, it appears to the eye as a very beautiful tree that is growing even while we stand and look at it. Downward pushes that part of the seed which becomes root; and the roots branch and branch again. Sometimes they encounter a buried stone; they pass around it, becoming crooked and devious, yet they never halt. Sometimes they encounter new soil, and thrust their way into it. Wherever they go, they draw from the soil what nourishment it offers. As they receive so they transmit to the tree; what the soil gives, the tree becomes.

Or shall we liken Christmas to the web in a loom? There are many weavers who work into the pattern the experience of their lives. When one generation goes, another comes to take up the weft where it has been dropped. The pattern changes as the mind changes, yet never begins quite anew. At first, we are not sure that we discern the pattern, but at last we see that, unknown to the weavers themselves, something has taken shape before our eyes; and that they have made something very beautiful, something which compels our understanding.

Yet to what can we really liken anything that is living and growing and changing, except to itself? When at last our figures fail us, we are turned back again to its own history; and strange indeed is that history, far beyond the imaginings of men and women.

It will tell us of an old, old Babylonian festival that moves westward, dividing its ways as it comes: through Greece into Rome as a festival that remodels itself at every step to fit the people among whom it settles; by another road into Israel, where at last it comes to rest beside the manger of Bethlehem; though not for long, since it then becomes part of the strength by which the faith of Christ conquered the entire pagan Mediterranean; and by yet another

route that skirts these other two: through the Balkans and up the Danube valley where, much disfigured and impoverished, it enters into the heathendom of the Northland. When last we shall view it, the Christian stream will have overtaken all others; and in the Northland the full-blown Christmas festival will have grown up as part of the very flesh and bone of Europe's many nations, and of those newer nations that have sprung up from them beyond the seas.

MILD BLOWS
THE SOUTH WIND

❧

EASTWARD OF THE ATLANTIC Ocean there is a sea whose waters are very blue under high white clouds. The lands facing it smile at the sun, and bring forth oranges, lemons, pomegranates, figs, dates. To the north, a great mountain rampart shuts them away from a darker country, where the summer's heat soon flies before the galloping cold.

In all the rest of the world there is no sea like the Mediterranean Sea. Around this body of water, and in the Tigris and Euphrates valleys to the east, many kinds of people have worked, played, thought, battled and sung as nowhere else. There humankind first turned grass into grains; there, too, perhaps, the first animals to carry loads and feed us from their flesh were made tame; there metals first became tools and weapons; there ships and cities and governments were invented. There the dark, clear eyes of priests first read the stately tale of the stars, and set forth on the greatest of all voyages of discovery: to seek the spirit who made the universe, who made the earth within the universe, who created the minds and bodies of people upon the earth.

Here was born, two thousand years ago, a boy whose mother was a peasant and whose cradle, says

 the story, was the feeding-trough of cattle. The story tells then of some Judean shepherds who beheld a wonderful vision deep in the night, and who arrived soon after with the first Christmas gift. It was lowly and perfect: they had nothing to offer him but their hearts in worship.

The story says, further, that some of those clear-eyed priests read in the stars of the infant and journeyed perilously to offer him gold, frankincense and myrrh.

Thus began a procession of men, women and children, lowly and noble. For over fifteen hundred years they have brought to this child the one marvelous and varied gift of Christmas. The sunny lands around the deep-blue waters of the Mediterranean have contributed their gilded domes and colored pillars and have made them into churches. To him they have given the garlands and boughs with which they once celebrated other gods.

There was another Wise Man, who did not arrive from the east, but from the north. This Wise Man came late, from the land of the swift summer and long, slow winter, from the endless forest of fir and spruce and juniper and oak. As we shall see, he came only after the mild south wind had brought him its message. Perhaps that is why he could not be included in the New Testament story, which closed centuries before he arrived.

Probably the Wise Men of the East would not have thought him rich, or even wise. In their day, he would have seemed even more uncouth and barbaric than the shepherds who had reached the manger first. But, in time, this other Wise Man too has brought his worship to the manger—gifts of stone flung high into space, in the slender shapes of solemn, pointed arches, and of glass colored to stain the light of the sun. Like the shepherd of Judea and the peasant of Italy, he has brought the gift of simple songs, songs that tramp the snowy streets on the silent, holy night, and enter into house and hall too lowly for vaulting stone and glowing window-glass.

The Wise Man of the North added also his old Yuletide—the boar's head which he took away from the feast of his old heathen god, Frey; his Yule log of Britain and Germany. He commissioned Saint Nicholas his master of ceremonies; he made the Christmas tree and set it up beside the manger.

The other Wise Men, with their gold, frankincense and myrrh, might not have thought much of these gifts; but they had left before the man of the Northland arrived. This man, who was a slow and painful thinker, who took a long time to become wise, conceived his gift over many centuries. Today we regard his gift as no less worthy than the treasure of the Magi. We know this gift as our own; for the Wise Man of the North—he is the people of the Northern Europe. Many of us own his blood; and all of us, whatever our blood, have come into his heritage.

"Dark and true and tender is the North." To the Mediterranean birthday of a Galilean peasant the Northland has brought the gifts of its forest and meadow.

THE RISING SUN GOES WEST

❦

A VERY OLD LEGEND of the Near East says that, far away in the mountains north of Mesopotamia, there is a Land of Eden, in which the waters under the earth well up and pour out as four great rivers; these diverge to feed life to all the parched world round about.

What the Land of Eden and its waters were to all the earth, the land of the Tigris and the Euphrates has been to our own way of life. Mesopotamia is the very ancient Mother of Civilization.

Christmas began there, over four thousand years ago, as the festival that renewed the world for another year. The "twelve days" of Christmas; the bright fires and probably the Yule log; the giving of presents; the carnivals with their floats, their merrymakings and clownings, the mummers who sing and play from house to house; the feastings; the church processions with their lights and song—all these and more began there centuries before Christ was born. And they celebrated the arrival of a New Year.

To the Mesopotamians, New Year's was a time of crisis. Once in a very distant time, their chief god Marduk (or Enlil, who is more ancient still than Marduk) had routed the monsters of chaos and had built out of a "world without form and void" an orderly world, and had created humankind. But the order remained an uneasy one: it ran down, so to speak, during the year; toward its close, after the crops had been harvested, the empty brown of the fields told that life was dying. Then  Marduk again had to do battle with the monsters of chaos, so that death might not become complete. Thus he renewed the world every year. It was a grim battle, fought in the regions below, and every time Marduk almost lost his struggle.

It was the duty of man, in his puny way, to help as well as he could; and much of the festival of the New Year constituted his lowly support of his god. His leader and commander was the king, who held his power and his title by the grace of the god.

As the Mesopotamians saw it, in the struggle of the New Year people faced a threefold problem: to purify themselves of the evils that their sins of the past year had brought upon them; to renew the strength that the year had drained away; and, if possible, to find a substitute who could take the consequences of the sins which they had committed.

The first and the last problems were solved by the notion of a "scapegoat," which is familiar to us from its form given in the Bible. Among the children of Israel it was prescribed that, on a certain day of the year, two goats should be brought before Jehovah's altar. There the high priest cast lots over them; one was sacrificed; on the other the high priest laid his hands in behalf of all the people, and so transmitted to its head all their sins of the year. This scapegoat was then led away into the wilderness and abandoned to the demon Azazel, who roamed there.

But in the present story we are concerned rather with what happened to the Babylonian king in this crisis when the world was dying. The New Year's festival lasted twelve days, as our Christmas season is supposed to do; in it the king repaired to Marduk's temple, to the court of the gods. The chief priest stripped from him his insignia of rank; thus dispossessed of his power, he knelt before Marduk's image and swore that he had done nothing against the god's will. The chief priest, now speaking for Marduk, said comforting words; and in the name of the god he reinvested the king, in token that the kingdom was restored to him by the grace of the god.

A very important part of the festival was the recitation of the Creation epic, the drama that re-enacted the creation of the world and its order by Marduk. There was also a darker side to the ceremony. In theory, the king must die at the end of the year; he should then accompany Marduk into the underworld and battle at his side, while a new king took his place on earth. But here enters the idea of a substitute or "mock" king, which saved the life of the real king. A criminal, real or fancied, was dressed in royal garb; he was given all the homage and indulgence that is the king's right, while the people about him held celebration. But soon his mock reign was over; he was stripped of his kingly trappings and slain in the place of the real king.

At last, as the festival went on, came the moment when Marduk began to prevail. The people, who had been supporting and encouraging him in the battle, turned to rejoicing. They joined processions of masqueraders. They drew wagons down the great avenue. They launched regattas on the Euphrates, with sham battles that were sometimes very realistic, to symbolize the fight of the god's forces with the dark powers of the deep.

There were other deeds which Europe still repeats during these holidays, although the ancient meanings have been lost: the building of bonfires in which a special wooden image of Marduk's opponent is burned; and the custom of exchanging visits and gifts.

This was *Zagmuk* festival. Another, which both Persians and Babylonians celebrated, was called the *Sacaea*. At this time, the masters and slaves exchanged places; the slaves commanded, the masters obeyed. One slave was chosen to be head of the household, and everyone paid homage to him.

The king's household celebrated on a larger and more intense scale, naturally, for the king stood for the nation. Two criminals who had been condemned to death were selected: one was set free; the other was dressed in royal clothes and constituted the make-believe king. The people paid him a mock homage, indulged his every whim, but, at last, they stripped him and scourged him and led him away to be crucified or hanged or beheaded.

As the old year died, the rules of ordinary living were relaxed. Then, as the new year arrived, the order of the world was recaptured. At this time of crisis, when fates hung in the balance, the curtain of the future was drawn slightly aside and, if you performed the proper magic, you could peer into it and make resolutions to fit coming events.

All peoples learned from this tremendous land of Mesopotamia. Everything happening there was in the course of time imitated by its neighbors—imitated, yet never copied exactly. Thus the rising sun traveled westward—through Greece to Rome. And it changed its face as it went.

There was another road too; and we are only beginning to appreciate that road which led from Asia Minor through the Balkans, up the Danube Valley into the heart of Europe. The Danubians were not like the Romans. When an idea from the Near East reached them, they fitted it into their scheme of living, in their own way. So it has come about repeatedly that one and the same basic idea has penetrated the Northland over at least two different routes: Rome and the Danube. There, in Northern Europe, it has, so to speak, caught up with itself wearing another guise. This is as true of Christmas as it is of many other things.

Marduk and his court of gods have long disappeared. But to this day in the Balkans and in Central Europe, on the twelve days of Christmas, troupes of masqueraders go about, headed by a "fool" or a "wild man"; also troupes of carol-singers, not unlike those we know from Merrie Olde England. As goes the weather of these days, so shall the months of the year. The girls still recite magic verses and perform magical acts to learn who their true-loves will be. There are still the bonfires, and a special log which a young man fells and brings home; and over this log a ritual is performed; and on Christmas Eve it is burned in the fireplace.

IO SATURNALIA!

THE RISING SUN WENT west, over Greece to Rome. In Greece there was an old god, Kronos, about whom we know little, even though it is not hard to recognize that his festival was the old *Sacaea* gone westward. The figures in the drama changed, the incidents also; but the plot remained. In ancient Babylonia, it was Marduk who conquered the monsters that lived before our world was created; in Greece, it was Zeus who fought and overcame Kronos and his Titans.

The Romans believed in an ancient god of seed-time, Saturn, who had ruled their country ages before their own day, before he was overthrown by Jupiter. Whenever the Romans thought that one of their gods resembled a Greek god, they concluded that the two were the same; then they took over the forms of worship that the Greeks already had observed. So Kronos came to Rome; the *Sacaea* entered into the *Saturnalia*.

The first day of the Saturnalia shifted during the lifetime of Rome; at all events, it began around the middle of December, with the cry, *Io Saturnalia!*—Ho Saturnalia!—and contin-  ued until January first. In its midst was December twenty-fifth, the day, as the Romans calculated, when the sun was at its lowest ebb, ready to increase again and impart its strength to the growing things of the earth. Hard upon this day came the *Calendae* of January—January first. The word itself has become the name that the Slavic and Baltic peoples use for the days of Christmas festivities; Koleda, Kolyada, Koledos, etc.

The Roman Saturnalia and the holidays that followed were boisterous indeed. Judging by what the Christians thought of them, they were often much worse than that. Very possibly the Christians had good reasons for their opinion. Today, however, some scholars are inclined to suspect that the Christians overdid their disapproval. Whatever the behavior of some Romans, others were simply merry, they masqueraded through the streets, ate big dinners, visited their friends, wished them good luck at this time of tender fortune, and gave each other good-luck gifts called *Strenae*. Originally, these were just lucky fruits. The Romans explained them as coming down from the time of King Tatius of the Sabines, who used to receive branches from a lucky tree

located in the grove of Strenae. Later on, the lucky fruits gave way to lucky cakes and other tokens of well-wishing.

The halls of the Romans were decked with boughs of laurel and of green trees, with lighted candles and with lamps—

for the hovering spirits of darkness were afraid of light. Masters and slaves ate together on these occasions, and sometimes they exchanged places, the masters waiting on the slaves. The slaves chose one of their number as leader of the household festival and as lord of the revel.

All this was harmless enough; but on the frontiers of the Roman Empire, on the Danube River and in the Balkans, much closer to the Near East, and much further from the influence of the mild south wind, the ancient customs stemming from Mesopotamia were hardly tamed at all. There is a story, quite possibly true, which tells how the Christian soldier, Dasius, became a martyr and a saint. Dasius belonged to the garrison of Dirostorum, which today is Silistra, Bulgaria—not far from where the Danube meets the Black Sea. When the Saturnalia arrived, the soldiers there chose by lot one among their number to be the Saturnine king of the revel. For thirty days they feted him, indulged him in all things, paid him rough and boisterous court. Then, when his thirty days were up, he had to stand at the altar and kill himself. In 303 AD, the lot fell upon Dasius, who refused to play pagan god for the amusement of his heathen comrades. The soldiers argued with him, and threatened his life, but Dasius would not give in. So they beheaded him. The sarcophagus of Saint Dasius reposes today in Ancona, Italy.

Io Saturnalia! To the pagans, the Saturnalia were fun. To the Christians, the Saturnalia were an abomination in homage to a disreputable god who had no existence anyway. The Christians, moreover, were dedicated to the slow, uphill task of converting these roistering pagan Romans. There were many immigrants into the ranks of the Christians by this time, but the Church Fathers discovered to their alarm that they were also facing an invasion of pagan customs. The habit of the Saturnalia was too strong to be left behind. At first the Church forbade it, but in vain. When a river meets a boulder that will not be moved, the river flows around it. If the Saturnalia would not be forbidden, let it be tamed. The Church Fathers now sought to point the festival toward the Christian Sun of Righteousness. If that could be done, the festival in its turn must of necessity grow worthy of him it celebrated.

On this account, some people have thought that the Christians invented Christmas to compete against the pagan celebrations of December twenty-fifth. For that day was sacred, not only to the pagan Romans but to a religion from Persia which, in those days, was one of Christianity's strongest rivals. This Persian religion was Mithraism, whose followers worshiped the sun, and celebrated its return to strength on that day. The Church finally succeeded in taking the merriment, the greenery, the lights, and the gifts from Saturn and giving them to the Babe of Bethlehem. Nevertheless, it would be shallow to conclude that this was all merely a clever trick. We must ask, rather, what, in those days, did New Year's and Christmas mean to the Christians?

To them, the most important thing that had ever happened in the world was the coming of Christ, his death, his resurrection. To them, it was all one big event, the beginning of a new era. They celebrated this event during that long interval between the dying of the old year, and the birth of the new and on into the spring; an old, old habit of centuries, but now richer and different in meaning.

But when had Christ's first coming taken place? We need not enter into the elaborate arguments by which the learned churchmen settled upon Decem-

ber twenty-fifth. It happened that the date did fall in the midst of the Satur- nalia. Far from being an invention to com- pete against Roman and Persian paganisms, the birthday of Christ ran the danger of being swallowed up in a pagan merry- making. The fathers tried strenuously to keep Christmas strictly a churchly celebration. It was part of their unremitting struggle to break the grip of the pagan gods upon the people. And they broke the grip—after a battle of centuries. The pagan Romans became Christian—but the Saturnalia remained.

A MOTHER AND CHILD
IN QUEST OF A BIRTHDAY

WHEN WAS JESUS BORN? No one knows. December twenty-fifth is no more the historical date of his birth than is any other. The Christians chose it to be his birthday only several centuries after he had lived and died.

The earliest Christians were not interested in Jesus' birthday, but by the fourth century they had become very much interested. How this came about is the story of a soil growing. Christmas is a seed that sprouted in that soil.

It sprouted when the Christians at last turned their eyes upon Jesus the infant and his mother Mary. There never would have been a Christmas as we know it without the Madonna and Child.

The Jesus whom we know from the early Gospel accounts walked among people and taught and blessed them. He loved small children. There is a Gospel story which says that once some adults brought their children to him, that they might know him. But his disciples would not have it so, and they stood in the way. Jesus was displeased at this, and said, "Let the children come to me; do not stand in their way; for the kingdom of God belongs to such as these."

Over the years that followed Jesus' death, the Christians tended to lose sight of him as the refuge of those who labor and are heavy-laden. What mattered most to them was that, at any moment, he would reappear to be the stern but righteous judge of all humankind. The world was to begin anew with a day of wrathful judgment.

To people who thought this way, the date of Jesus' physical birth could not matter. To celebrate it would have seemed at best pointless, and at worst an evil thing. By the third century, however, many people were coming to the notion that his birthday should be observed (if only they could be sure when that was); yet in 245 AD the great Church father, Origen, declared it to be a sin even to think of keeping the birth-day of Christ, "as though he were a king Pharaoh."

Many early Christians refused to believe that so divine a being could have been born at all; and they invented ingenious ways for explaining away the Gospel stories.

Although we cannot plunge into the arguments by which the Church finally arrived at the conclusions that made Christmas possible, very briefly, the steps are these: in some ways, the Church was sure, Christ was divine; but how? If he was divine, could he be human also? Could he be both divine and human without having his divineness sullied by his humanness? The tradition of the Gospels claimed him to be the Messiah of Jewish prophecy, whose birth should be from the line of King David. But how authoritative were the Gospels, and just what did they mean? If divine nature cannot partake of human nature without being sullied, and Jesus was divine, then either the Gospels were allegory or, at best, not to be taken literally. The true Christ therefore must have walked the earth unborn and not truly of the flesh.

There was an opposite and widespread belief that he was born entirely and only human; but that, when at last he was baptized by John in the Jordan River, the spirit of God descended into him and he became divine also. If so, then his *human* birth still was unimportant; but his *divine* birth—at *baptism*—was very important. In the early Church, the day of his baptism—Epiphany, January sixth—was a great festival.

Our Christmas depends upon the fact that, after a severe struggle, the Church repudiated the notion that Jesus had never been born at all; and somewhat later, the idea that he became divine only at his birth.

Oddly, then, the fact that we have a Christmas depends at this critical point upon what the Christians of the second and third centuries decided about baptism. Originally, only people who had reached the age of discretion could be baptized. In this later time, baptism was pushed forward until it was bestowed upon infants; they, too, should have their portion in the Kingdom of Christ.

And the Church decided that Christ had been *born* divine. He had not received his divinity on his baptism. A God-infant, yet a human-infant, too, born of a human mother. Divinity in an infant. God's grace in every child. The two went together.

By at least the third century, Jesus' birthday was being celebrated at various times, even as late as April. January sixth was favored, since on that day, too, he is supposed to have been baptized when he had at last reached manhood. In the church of the oldest Christian nation of all—the Armenian—it still is the day of Christmas. Now we are prepared to understand one of the chief reasons why the day of baptism and the day of nativity were separated, and Christ's birthday became a church festival completely in its own right. But precisely why December twenty-fifth was chosen would lead us again into a swamp; that of the queer astronomical and legendary speculations that clustered about the calendar of those early Christian centuries. At all events, it was not in the East but in the West that this Feast of the Nativity first took hold on December twenty-fifth. Either by 336 AD or about 353 AD, it was so celebrated in Rome. Then it spread eastward, until it embraced almost the entire Christian church.

The thoughts of people had been changing. This is the same century in which we find Christians regarding Mary the mother of Jesus in a new light. She had long been revered, along with the other saints and apostles; but *only* along with them. But now, in this same fourth century, we see her emerging as the Queen of Heaven. The Divine Christ had been born both human and divine, of a human mother. Mary had done a thing which certainly no other woman had done. This in itself set her off from all other humanity; but there is something deeper than this bald fact. For Mary represented something that the human heart ached for, and the ache was not being solaced.

The Gospels told of a Son of Man who walked in the sun and dust of the roads of Palestine. He healed the hurts of the people, the hurts of body and soul. He called to himself those who labored and were heavy-laden, and promised them refreshment that no earthly power could give. But his followers could not keep in mind at once this Jesus and the stern judge who sat on a throne in heaven and who would some day return in glory to deal an even-handed justice to all humankind. It was a renewal of the world  in this latter way, and not a renewal of the heart in the former way, which won.

So the heart's ache remained. It became the burden of Mary.

At Chartres, France, there is a cathedral with an apse whose beauty must be seen to be believed. And here, as Henry Adams writes in *Mont Saint-Michel and Chartres*, "we see, and the artist meant that we should see, only the great lines, the color, and the Virgin. The mass of suppliants before the choir look up to the light, clear blues and reds of this great space, and feel there the celestial peace and beauty of Mary's nature and abode. There is heaven! and Mary looks down from it, into her church, where she sees us on our knees, and knows each of us by name. There she actually is—not a symbol or in fancy, but in person, descending on her errands of mercy and listening to each one of us, as her miracles prove, or satisfying our prayers merely by her presence which calms our excitement as that of a mother calms her child. She is there as a Queen, not merely as an intercessor, and her power is such that to her the difference between us earthly beings is nothing. . . . People who suffer beyond the formulas of expression—who are crushed into silence, and beyond pain—want no display of emotion—no bleeding heart—no weeping at the foot of the cross—no hysterics—no phrases! They want to see God, and know that He is watching over His own. How many women are there, in this mass of thirteenth century suppliants, who have lost children? Probably nearly all, for the death rate is very high in the conditions of medieval life. There are thousands of such women here, for it is precisely this class who come most; and probably every one of them has looked up to Mary in her great window and has felt actual certainty, as though she saw with her own eyes—there, in heaven, while she looked—her own lost baby playing with the Christ-child at the Virgin's knee, as much at home as the saints, and much more at home than the kings. Before rising from her knees, every one of those women will have bent down and kissed the pavement in gratitude for Mary's mercy."

The cathedral of Chartres is the fruit from many centuries of a growing faith; the faith that was building Christmas. The same centuries and the same people who made of the birthday of a divine-human infant a beautiful and tremendous church festival, brought into being new festivals in worship of Mary the Virgin Mother.

At this late hour in history, on the eve of the millennium, it is very hard for us to recapture any measure of that first, fine ecstasy that came from the sudden conviction that God had at last come to dwell among men and women and the world had begun anew. It was strong enough to date all our years henceforth as BC or AD. It was more than a matter of the year; to the early churchmen, Year One began with December twenty-fifth.

And no matter what our creed, we can afford to pause for a moment before as sublime and daring a thought as has ever crossed the intellect of men and women: that on a certain December twenty-fifth, God condescended to appear on earth in the guise of a human baby, of a human mother, a simple Jewish peasant woman, who ushered him in under the old, old burden of women the world over, and in that common place where, in the Near East, many peasant babies were and still are ushered into the world: a stable or some other outbuilding.

It is a thought that for centuries the minds of ignorant and educated alike have striven to comprehend. How they have striven, and how in their utmost they have yet realized that they have never quite comprehended, is written in the record of the jewel-covered Bambino in the manger that stands in the Italian churches at Christmas time; in the hymns of the Greek and the Latin churches; in the Ave Maris Stella, the Stabat Mater, the Ave Maria, in the quaint fancies of the carols from Bohemia, Flanders, the Tyrol; the dramatic reenacting, at Christmas time, both in church and marketplace, of the Gospel stories of the Nativity; and the many, many pictures and statues of the Madonna and Child that have come down the years to tell us how mightily a great thought had seized upon the faith of our forebears.

THE SCHOOLING
OF THE NORTHLAND

NEITHER FRONTIER GARRISONS NOR mountain ramparts that shut away the Mediterranean coastlands from the northlands could protect Rome forever. Eventually the dike was broken; the barbarian invaders flowed through.

They came on foot, on horseback, in heavy wagons—tribes of Germans, Slavs, Finns; men, women, children—all crowding to find some place within that sunny southland from which had drifted fabulous tales of life's ease and richness. Rome could not absorb all who came. Rome died; the Christian Church lived.

From the ruins of its homeland, the Church sent forth an army of missionaries into town, hamlet, camp, to persuade those who had conquered and destroyed that they yet had not conquered, that there was a more excellent way of life. No one can read the record of these men without being amazed, not only at their heroism, but at their audacity; for they stood up to the conquerors—men who spoke with a sword of tempered iron—and, in another language, actually convinced them that their greatest victory would not come until they had submitted to the very power they imagined they had vanquished.

These pioneering missionaries have left a few records of themselves; and, though they were written twelve to fifteen hundred years ago, to us who know the story of an American frontier only recently left behind, they are strange, yet familiar; for they tell of endless forests, somber, cold mountains, wild animals, and very simple humans in countries where today there are paved highways and farmsteads and cities.

Here begins the schooling of the Northland.

Even before the missionaries brought the ideas of Christian Rome to them, the Germanic peoples had learned a good deal from pagan Rome. The missionaries were aware of this, but they did not know that the Near East had long influenced those Germanic peoples via the Balkans and the Danube valley. For instance, the masquerading mummers and even Saint Nicholas himself may first have reached the heart of Europe not from the south but from the southeast. Nor could the missionaries realize that this influence would continue unbroken all the while they were striving to convert the pagans of Northern Europe.

What did the pagan Germans know or believe when the missionaries reached them? They knew that winter followed upon summer, and that spring followed upon winter, that winter was the time when nature's green life died away, except in the evergreens. It was then, they believed, that spirits of darkness howled across the fields and through the forests, and wrenched at the eaves and broke into barns and stables. The Germans knew the moods of earth and air, but little about the habits of the stars;

they had no way of measuring the solstice and equinox until they learned of them from the Romans. They were also glad to learn of the Romans' Saturnalia.

There exists a letter from the year 742 AD, in which Saint Boniface, the "Apostle to the Germans," complains to Pope Zacharias that his labors to convert the heathen Franks and Alemans—Germanic tribes—were being handicapped by the escapades of the Christian Romans back home. The Franks and the Alemans were on the threshold of becoming Christians, but their conversion was retarded by their enjoyment of lurid carnivals. When Boniface tried to turn them away from such customs, they argued that they had seen them celebrated under the very shadow of Saint Peter's in Rome. Embarrassed and sorry, Pope Zacharias replied to Boniface, admitting that the people in the city of Rome misbehaved very badly at Christmas time. There was very little he could do about it; however, the following year he succeeded in inducing the Holy Synod of Rome to forbid the Romans, under penalty, from setting such bad examples.

Alas for human frailty! The ban had to be repeated over and over, for centuries.

Out in the Northland, how well did the missionaries succeed? Let us look at Christmas in the Middle Ages, particularly in the mid-fifteenth century. Holly, ivy and evergreens were up, candles and torches were lit, and mummers clowned in the streets. There were singers, Christmas presents, fortunetelling and much feasting and drinking. The people chose, not a mock king, but a "Lord of Misrule," an "Abbot of Unreason," a "King of the Bean," a "Pope" who presided over the "Feast of the Fools" or the "Feast of the Asses." They made him a bald-

headed, red-nosed clown, and set him on a donkey. He had a retinue; like hoboes on a spree, these ancestors of ours squawked an "anthem," danced about the donkey, and hied themselves to the church or cathedral where they performed a slapstick mass. The choir was vested in tatters or in robes turned inside out; they wore orange peels for spectacle rims; they held their musicsheets upside down and jangled a gibberish response to the "bishop" who read the service. They rang the bells, they hop-skip-jumped through the church. *Io Saturnalia! Ho, Golden Age of Kronos! Hail Sacaea!*

But it would be unfair to leave the picture this way. As difficult as it was to tame the Saturnalia, it was being done. Today the boughs are up, the Christmas dinner is on, the gifts and greeting cards are on the table and the floor. The pageants remain, the carols and the church services. The songs are no less gay; yet their notes are richer and humbler, for they tell the story of a Mother and Child who at last have found a birthday.

THE RAGING ROUT
OF THE TWELVE NIGHTS

TO THE OLD PAGANS of Northern Europe, the year began with winter; but what they called winter included our late autumn. By October or November, the harvest is in, the cattle are bedded down. It is time to thank the gods for the store of the barn and the stable. Sometimes our harvest is poor, sometimes we have enough; we seldom have more. Ahead stretch the long months of snow, with barely the feed on hand for the cattle and the swine. It is wiser to thin out the herds now, or risk having all the animals starve later. In late November, therefore, or early December, we must slaughter the extra animals and preserve the meat. It is a good time to invite friends in for a bit of feasting. But before we begin, we must thank the gods—Thor, Odin, Njörd, Frey—by offering them some of the meat, too, and by drinking beer or mead to them, and may they grant to our labors in the new year a goodly reward.

The god who cared for the fertile herd was Frey, after whom Friday is named; his animal symbol was the boar.

Even after the pagan gods had passed on, the boar sacrifice was too enjoyable to be forgotten. It still survives in the feast of Merrie Olde England in which the boar is treated as if it were some royal personage—first  the trumpets blow, the door swings open, in marches a platter bearing a steaming boar's head, an apple in its mouth; behind it troops a procession of lusty puddings. Cheers and laughter from the spectators poised to attack it—valiant trenchermen whose an-

cestors worshiped Frey but of whom they themselves probably never have heard. This too is
Christmas.

Wednesday, literally, is *Woden's Day;* and once
Woden was chief among the Northland gods.

As Germanic gods go, Woden was not very
ancient; for he wandered into the beliefs of the people about the time that Christ was born. From the
Near East, he made his way northward into Scandinavia, where his name was pronounced *Odin.*

How Odin became the chief of the Germanic
gods we do not know for certain; written records of
those days are very few. At any rate, when the Germanics adopted him they acquired some new and
more exalted ideas of what a god could or should be.
For gradually Odin grew into a very wise god who
knew everything that was going on in the world. On
each of his shoulders perched a sharp-eyed, wag-
tongued raven who flew forth to the ends of the
earth and came back to prattle on about everything it
saw. Sometimes Odin himself toured the world on
his white horse, Sleipnir, who had eight legs to give
him greater speed. At other times Odin preferred to

hike, wrapped in his blue cloak and wearing his broad-brimmed hat, carrying his wanderer's staff.

The Northmen knew the icy shadow of the Arctic, the rage and gloom of a nature far different from that of the mild south wind and the blue Mediterranean. In the North of Europe, eternal vigilance and struggle were the price of safety and shelter. While the scribes of Mesopotamia might feel secure with Marduk to champion them, the Norse poet-philosophers were driven to believe that even people and gods together could not hold back forever the dark, grim giants of nature. The giants were only biding their time. Some day the uneasy truce between them and the gods would snap. The giants would advance to settle for all time their ancient grudge. Then Odin would be forced to marshal the gods and their allies quickly to meet this Day of Judgment, for over them Fate had already pronounced sentence. Who, at this time, would be the gods' allies? They would be men who had proven on the battlefield that they were worthy to fight under the waning but unyielding banners of the gods: slain warriors whose spirits had been recruited into Valhalla against that day. Thus did Odin become god of the warriors.

Within a few brief centuries after Odin captured the loyalty of the Northmen, a milder God with a quieter strength and a better hope deposed him; but during those centuries, Odin himself grew into a finer godhood. That is why he has never really faded out, and why he comes into our Christmas story. Although he never ceased to be the leader of armed and wild hosts, he rose to a mildness and a concern for humankind. Even before they were converted to the religion of Christ, the Germanic peoples heard rumors or garbled tales about it; and some

of the things they heard and thought they under-stood were transferred to the legend of their Odin.

Perhaps this explains why they began calling Odin "All-Father"; why they made him the chief god in a pagan trinity of their own, a trinity that became the creator of humankind. Moreover, they told the story about how Odin once made a sacrifice of him-self. For nine nights (the Germanics counted time by "nights" rather than by "days") he dedicated himself by hanging on a tree, pierced by a spear; which may recall one who hung upon a cross until the ninth hour. At the end of that time, Odin received a drink of mead; then he cried out—*the letters of the Northmen's alphabet, the runes!* Thus, they believed, was writing invented. To the Northmen, these scars which could be scratched on wood or stone, so that forever after-ward they could speak silently to whoever was versed in their mystery, were no less than a revelation; one which only a god could capture, and only by submit-ting to a great and deep pain.

Because Odin saw all with his one eye, and knew all, and wished the world well, he grew to be a just god. At times, he even became gruffly kind. He seemed to move everywhere, in the daily affairs of people. But though he increased in stature, he did not grow away from his more ancient guises. The German *Schimmelreiter* (Rider of the White Horse), old *Schlapphut* (Flapping Hat, the Wide-Awake), still rides the storms on his white horse, wearing his hat and his fluttering mantle. In Scandinavia they still say, *Oden jagar förbi*—Odin is riding past. But his rout of warriors, recruited into Valhalla against the final judgment-battle, have ceased to be fancied as warriors; they have become demons and executed criminals. *Wodenes her* means Woden's army. By people who no longer knew what this meant, it was twisted to *wütendes Heer*, a phrase that still lives, and which we translate as "raging rout."

The raging rout arrives about the time of Halloween, to stay in the country throughout the winter. It comes with Woden at its head, or with a harridan named Holda or Perchta or Berchtel. If the rout comes on a soft wind, the next year will be goodly; if the rout comes raging, the year will be hapless and full of warfare. It is the season when fortunes are revealed. The visitors are awaited anxiously—wagon and plow must be hidden; the women hasten to finish their spinning, that the distaff may be empty, the wheel at rest, and a fair stock of yarn laid by. If it is Perchta who comes, she inspects the household on the night of Saint Nicholas, December sixth. The housewife sets the table with a meal for her, that she may grant her approval to the record of the house; for Perchta is stern and punishes the lazy.

In America, the witches of Halloween have turned into small and very human pranksters. But in the countryside of Europe, the raging rout remains much more formidable. Over there, we find clowns and buffoons who are full-grown fellows out for plenty of rough horseplay. The farmer does well to hide his wagon and plow and everything else that might be a handle for mischief.

As we trace the roots that Woden has struck into the life of the Germanic peoples, we find him turning up in the most unexpected places. For instance, in the *Nibelung-enlied*, the great German epic of the twelfth century, he has shrunk to the stature of a legendary king in a land no longer pagan. Again, he has merged into the legend of the great king who has never died but now sleeps inside a mountain while the ravens fly about outside, a king who will wake up some day, when his nation needs his help to fight off the enemy. Of most interest to us, however, is the fact that Woden has become—Santa Claus, or, as he is more accurately called, Saint Nicholas.

It is obvious, then, that Woden has an amazing capacity for becoming someone else, or for merging with someone else to make a new person. In Europe, in contrast to America, Saint Nicholas wears a broad-brimmed hat and rides his faithful old white horse. His comrades have now dwindled to four: his brother, Rupert, who goes along with a switch to take care of the children who do not deserve what Saint Nicholas has in his bag; the Christ Child; Saint Peter; and an angel. When he enters the house, he sits down and gives the children something of an examination; have they learned their lessons? their proper prayers? have they done their errands cheerfully? If they pass, he rewards them from his pack. In some places in Europe he does not come on Christmas Eve as he does in America, but on the eve of December sixth.

But who was the "real" Saint Nicholas?

GOD INTO SAINT

WE KNOW ALMOST NOTHING about the man who some day was to become "Saint" Nicholas. He lived during the reigns of the Roman Emperors, Diocletian, Maximilian, Constantine, late in the third century and into the fourth. His parents were well-to-do Christians of a province of Asia Minor. When he was still a young man, Nicholas was consecrated Archbishop of Myra, a seaport town. He died in 326 AD, on December sixth.

He must have been a remarkable person, judging by the varied and numerous legends that have gathered about his life on earth and his life as a saint after his death. In the last hundred years or so, he has branched out from Europe into new territory, until now he has adopted all the children in the United States. But while his job in America occupies his time only once a year, across the ocean his work lasts all the year around.

In fact, he is probably the hardest-working saint of all. It would take volumes to tell of all of his deeds and adventures from one end of Europe to the other. From England to Greece to Russia, he rides the storm at sea, saving the lives of sailors for whom he is the last and only help. In days gone by, neither Greek nor Russian mariners would weigh anchor without an icon of Saint Nicholas in the forecastle. The Venetian sailors, inbound or outbound, always stopped at an island outside the city to invoke or thank him. His churches dot the coast of England, almost four hundred of them—more in number even than those of England's patron, Saint George.

Far from the sea, the Balkan Slavs know him as the rescuer of ships, and on his day they prepare carp by a special recipe. When he comes riding on his wings, the storm dies. There is a folk song of the Serbians and Bulgarians that says that once all the saints gathered to drink wine on a pleasant little social occasion. Saint Basil went around with a golden jug, and each saint filled his golden cup. They talked away; but Saint Nicholas began to nod, and his cup tilted in his hand. All the other saints stopped to watch him. Saint John asked, "Brother Nicholas, why are you dozing with a cup in your hand?" And Saint Nicholas roused himself and replied, "Saint John, since you ask—the enemy had raised a terrible storm in the Aegean Sea; so, while my body dozed here, my spirit was off to rescue all the ships and bring them to shore."

By saving ships at sea, Saint Nicholas saves the landlubber merchants who are their passengers. Therefore, since he protects merchants at sea, surely

he protects them on land as well. By this reasoning, he becomes the patron saint of travelers everywhere, protecting their goods, and insuring them safe passage. Even pirates, being sailors, claimed his protection.

Moreover, if he is master of the storm, then surely he can bring it on as well as cause it to abate. In fact, some who have studied the Saint Nicholas stories believe that the same beliefs the Roman and Greek sailors held about their gods of the sea, Neptune and Poseidon, have been transferred by Christian sailors to Saint Nicholas.

He is also the special saint of numerous places, particularly in Russia. The Russians adopted him when, almost a thousand years ago, they became Christianized. But Saint Nicholas has tremendous energy; he has traveled northward across all of Russia, and overleaped the frontiers of Christianity itself to become the helper of the pagan Samoyed and Laplanders—the people of the reindeer, the fishermen of the Arctic Ocean. In America, we tend to believe that the Arctic is his one and only residence.

Saint Nicholas is the protector of all humble and small folk. He is special guardian of unmarried girls. Legend says that while Nicholas was still a young man, his parents died and left him two things: a substantial fortune, and a strange and impractical conscience. The Scriptures say, "When thou doest alms, let not thy left hand know what thy right hand doeth, that thine alms may be in secret." Nicholas found himself faced with the problem of giving away his fortune to the needy without letting them know whence it came.

However, he had been solving it very well when, one day, he chanced to be passing the house of a nobleman, a widower. This man had three marriageable daughters, but no longer anything with which to feed and clothe them, much less a dowry for each of them. And without dowries no one would marry them. The times were desperate; there seemed no other solution than to sell the girls one by one into slavery. Nicholas overheard father and daughters lamenting together. Of his once-great fortunes he still had three bags of gold left. That night, he returned to the nobleman's house with one of his bags, and dropped it through a small window. Thus it came about that the eldest daughter found a husband.

Soon it was the turn of the second daughter: again Nicholas slipped a bag of gold through the window, in the dead of night, and thus won for her a husband.

The father now expected, apparently, that all good things come in threes; for this time he hid himself in ambush. Nicholas did indeed appear, in the night, with his third bag of gold and tossed it into the room through the little window. Then, as he fled, the father ran after him, and caught hold of his clothes, and threw himself on his knees. "Oh, Nicholas, servant of God," he cried, "why hide thy good deeds thus?" But Nicholas enjoined him to tell no one.

Once, after Nicholas had become Archbishop, a nobleman sent his young sons on a long journey to Myra so that Nicholas might give them his blessing. On the way, they stopped overnight at a hostelry.

While they slept the inn-keeper stole into their room and murdered them and then stripped them of their money and their goods. But God sent word to Nicholas in a vision; and he arose  quickly, sought out the innkeeper and confronted him with his crimes. The innkeeper was terrified; he fell at the Archbishop's feet and implored to be for-given. So Nicholas prayed, and God raised up the boys to life again.

These two legends reveal to us something of the figure who one day was to become Santa Claus; for here we see him as the protector of children and of helpless young girls. He has already developed the habit of slipping gifts into the homes of worthy people in the dark of night. But the lore of the com-mon folk is always prone to take the most unexpect-ed turns. Nicholas the saint is often pictured with the three bags of gold; but usually these bags have taken on the shape of three balls. After the mer-chants had adopted him as watch and ward over their worldly goods, the three golden dowries of the nobleman's daughters became—the symbol of the pawnbroker! A man's goods, that is, are safe under the sign of Saint Nicholas.

The schools of the Middle Ages were connected with monasteries. There the boys were encouraged by their teachers to act plays and pageants about the life of the saint who was fond of them. The boys took their parts very seriously. Early in the tenth century, the king of Germany Conrad I, tells of visiting a monastery while the boys were in the midst of their Saint Nicholas celebration. They were "Bishop Nicholas" and his churchly retinue, filing solemnly up the aisle of the church. The king was much amused. He told his followers to toss apples to them—but the earnest procession never swerved. It passed on; the apples lay where they had fallen.

Eventually the processions by which the schoolboys honored their patron saint on his day, moved out of the monasteries into the streets of the cities. On December sixth, the children chose a Boy Bishop and constituted themselves his retinue. They trooped through the neighborhood, collecting tribute from the burghers; and on to the cathedral, where their "bishop" actually entered the chancel, took part in the real church service, and even delivered a sermon. The children's revel lasted until December twenty-eighth—Holy Innocents, the day commemorating King Herod's slaughter of all the infant boys of Judea after the Wise Men had told him that a new "king" had been born in his country.

This broad pageantry has faded over the years, and not much more remains than the custom for children to roam about with switches, levying their tribute from house to house. Yet we are not as far from the days of the full pageant as we might think: in Austria, for instance, Saint Nicholas still appears on his day, traveling about in robes and miter—certainly not in the familiar scarlet jacket and breeches with white fleece trimmings.

And this is how a god turns into a saint. Both Woden and Saint Nicholas are travelers of the road; they wander afoot and on horseback, inspecting the deeds of humankind, making sure that right and order prevail. They do this when the days of the year are shortest, when a new year is on its way, when the fortunes of the future are being cast. Both of them ride the storm; they can subdue it or they can rouse it. They have ended up by becoming the same person.

So, when the children of the Lower Rhineland, on both sides of the Dutch-German border, set out their clogs for "Santeklas" (there are many versions of the name Saint Nicholas) to fill on the eve, not of December twenty-fifth, but of December sixth, they put hay in them for the white horse, and their parents set out a sheaf of grain. Woden's horse or Nicholas'—it is all one. Sometimes, instead of clogs, they would set out little wooden ships, in honor of the mariner-saint. But, clogs or ships, they always place them by the chimney, for this saint through many centuries has preferred to deliver his presents secretly in the night.

GREEN IS OUR SHIELD

WHEN THE HARVEST HAS been laid away, and brown death has driven off the summer's green, and nightly frosts lay a brittle lace over the countryside, and the white snow brings back to us the foothills of the Arctic, then the raging rout comes riding. There is no defense against it but the living green of summer.

Box, bay, ivy, holly, yew, larch, juniper, pine, spruce, fir—all are shields against the witches and the demons. The spines of the hollyleaves become thickets to catch and hold the hags; juniper-smoke is a demon-chasing incense. In the Tyrol, for instance, even city people smoke misfortune out of their houses, while the farmer carries smouldering sprigs in a brazier, along with a bowl of holy water, into every room and crevice, into the stalls of the cattle, onto the threshing floor. Every animal is censed and besprinkled; so, too, the beds of the girls and the doors to their chambers. As the houseman makes his rounds he keeps saying, "In with the good luck; out with the bad." Finally, all of the people of the household gather in a circle, and each receives from the master a "smoke blessing."

All the Northland cherishes the greens that do not die. "Against the Feast of Christmas every man's house, as also their parish churches, were decked with holly, ivy, bay, and whatsoever the season of the year afforded to be green. The conduits and standards in the streets were likewise garnished." According to John Stow's *The Survey of London*, such was the city in the fifteenth century.

Weapons against the weird and ghostly vermin were not only greenery, evergreen incense and lights, but noise; shouts, horns, bells, even banging guns, especially on New Year's Day. During the Twelve Days of Christmas (or Twelve Nights, if we reckon in the old Germanic way) you must avoid heavy work as much as possible, lest you be tripped up by one of these invisible evil-wishers; and you must not eat peas or beans. On the other hand, a broom a day sweeps the witches away, so bind a new broom on each of the twelve. As in Rome and Babylon, the Twelve Days are full of augury for the twelve months of the coming year—to each of the Twelve Days its month of the same order. You may learn what the weather and the growing season are going to be by noting the sun, wind, rain, and snow on each of the twelve days; you may also learn your own fortune for the year if you go through the proper magic acts. The green boughs can bring you luck, too, if someone switches you with them. Thus it is a good time—among Slavs as well as Germanics—for the children to collect gifts from the neighbors by going around and switching them with green boughs and reciting good-luck ditties.

Why do the winter demons fear the greens? Green belongs in the realm of summer and life; winter kills most of summer's train, but the greens remain steadfast. Where the greens are, it is not winter. They are the enemies of winter's white death.

Although "Christ's Mass" covers twelve days, strictly speaking, the power of winter's demons remains until Candlemas, February second. By that time the days are lengthening, the sun endures longer. The winter has allowed many demons to find shelter in the nooks and crannies of the house; only a continuous struggle with lights and greenery and

incense has kept them within bounds; and now the spring is about to begin, and none of these wintry denizens must be allowed to overstay to spoil the early sprouts. Therefore, on Candlemas, many candles are lighted to blaze at the demons, and the people bear these lights in a great procession.

A CHRISTMAS CALENDAR

CHRIST'S MASS COVERS TWELVE days, and those twelve days are the climactic part of a broader season. Although the various bodies of Christians do not agree in all details, roughly and in main features the Christmas season goes thus:

November eleventh is Saint Martin's Day, and calls for special bonfires. About this time occurs the first of four Advent Sundays, looking to the "advent" of the Babe at midnight of Christmas Eve.

December sixth is Saint Nicholas' Day. The old saint comes to make ready for the Master's coming. In Europe, this is the day when he visits the houses, and brings presents for the good children and a switch for the bad. In some places he brings the

Christmas tree. Between this date and Christmas proper, the children troop about town. They carry good-luck switches, which they use upon their elders, and collect gifts in return.

December twenty-fourth is Christmas Eve.

December twenty-fifth is Christmas Day.

December twenty-eighth is Holy Innocents—in commemoration of the infant boys whom Herod slaughtered in his vain attempt to include the new-born "King of the Jews."

January first is New Year's Day.

January sixth is Epiphany—the day when the Magi visited the manger, and also the day of Jesus'

baptism at the beginning of his ministry. (The name itself derives from this occasion.) By this day the "twelve days of Christmas" are over, and the tree should be down.

February second is Candlemas (in America, it is often known as "ground-hog day"), when the greenery of the winter season should come down, and candles and fires are lit.

THE TREE

❧

WHENCE CAME THE CHRISTMAS tree, and when did it arrive?

Mystery blurs the true answer. There have been so many speculations about its origins that it is best to clear away some of the false ideas that have concealed whatever of fact is really known.

To the collection of false ideas we may at once assign the widespread notion that Martin Luther was out walking one night, and the stars suggested to him lights, which he then placed upon a fir tree to brighten the Christmas of his son. Nor can a good case be made for the Yule log as the ancestor of the Christmas tree. One favorite notion has been that it is the symbol of the Tree of Life, which stood in the

Garden of Eden. Indeed, in the eighteenth and nineteenth centuries, in northern Germany, that is precisely the way people regarded it; in Hamburg, for instance, you could buy little figurines of Adam and Eve and the serpent, to place under the tree. But this idea attached itself to the tree late in its history, and then only in a region where the tree had not originated. The reason for this mistake is worth recording.

December twenty-fourth, in the medieval church calendar, was Adam-and-Eve's Day. On this day, the people play-acted the legends of the Garden of Eden; and before the show, the actors trooped through the town, with Adam carrying the Tree of Life, on which apples were hung.

What makes it so hard to state certainly just when and where and how the Christmas tree came into being is the fact that the precise event was never written down. Furthermore, the veneration of some particular tree as being the property or the dwelling of a spirit was so widespread and so varied among the pagan Europeans that the customs which grew up about it have provided a wide range for those who like to make guesses. We do not have to go back far in time to see the peasants of Europe setting up and decorating trees on almost every important holiday. The Maypole itself was a tree, and it even bore the same ornaments that were used on the Christmas tree; but garnished trees stood also on Shrovetide, Palm Sunday, Easter, Ascension Day, Harvest Home (called the "harvest may"), Saint Martin's, Saint Nicholas', New Year's, and even others. If the tree of Christmas in particular belongs to this family, then somehow, and unaccountably, it is a lone survivor.

We do know that the tree is part of what the common people contributed to Christmas; the Church not only did not create it, but frowned upon it when it first came to attention. Even as late as the 1740s, the Reverend Johann Konrad Dannhauer, of Strassburg, had this to say: "Among other trifles with which the people often occupy the Christmas time more than with God's word, is also the Christmas or fir tree, which they erect in the house, and hang with dolls and sugar and thereupon shake and cause to lose its bloom. Where the habit comes from, I know not. It is a bit of child's play. . . . Far better were it for the children to be dedicated to the spiritual cedar tree, Jesus Christ." In this the Roman clergy were at one with the Protestant pastor.

There are many accounts of Christmas festivities going back into the Middle Ages; but they never mention the Christmas tree. A forest ordinance from Ammerschweier in Alsace, dated 1561, says that no burgher "shall have for Christmas more than one bush of more than eight shoes' length." This seems to be the first mention of anything that can be rec-

ognized as the tree. In a travel book, dated 1605, there is this passage: "At Christmas time in Strassburg they set up fir trees in the rooms, and they hang on them roses cut of many-colored paper, apples, wafers, gilt, sugar, and so on. They make around them a four-cornered space, and in front—" here the lines fade out.

The Tree Hangs

Briefly and simply, the Christmas tree seems to have sprung from the devil-defying green with which longstanding tradition of the Northland had decorated house and barn at New Year's.

The greens sometimes took the form of a tree-tip hung from the rafters. In some places this still is the custom. In Styria, Austria, as in other Roman Catholic lands, the tip of a fir or a spruce, decorated with red strips of paper, apples, and gilded nuts, is hung upside down in the corner of the living room, known as the "Lord God's Corner." Even as late as the mid-nineteenth century, in Germany there were other ways of hanging "Christ's tree"—in the window, from the rafters of the room, with tip upward, the butt sharpened, and an apple suspended under it—while the whole tree was dressed with paper, tin stars, cakes, apples, candles. As late as 1890, in some places the tree was hung over the doorway, upside down, without lights, but colorfully decorated.

The Tree Blooms

In her treasure chest of folklore, the Church keeps the story that on the first Noel the world awoke to sing as it had never done before. The animals in their stalls began to talk to each other; in defiance of the snow and the night's darkness, trees put forth blossoms and fruits; the heavens shed a healing dew, and the rivers and walls turned to wine. This story the priests never tired of relating to the people; at last it came to be believed that the miracle repeated itself, in rare places, every Christmas Eve. Some of the more rugged spirits among the folk used to go where such trees or bushes were said to be, and watch through the night for the marvelous bloom.

This power was a rare and special heritage. In an Alsatian village, says one legend, there is a rose that does not bloom in the time of roses; on the night of the Nativity alone it comes to flower and glows afar, for it is a stock from the bush on which Mary hung her baby's swaddling-clothes while on her flight into Egypt. To Glastonbury, says another legend, came Joseph of Arimathea, he in whose tomb Jesus had been laid away, and who brought the Holy Grail to England. There he planted his staff, and settled down; there he died. The staff rooted and became a thorn-tree. Slips from this bush were transplanted to other spots in the neighborhood, and the thorn always came into full bloom on Christmas Day.

In the year 1752, England changed over from the Julian ("Old Style") to the Gregorian ("New Style") calendar, and September second became September fourteenth. This, of course, advanced December twenty-fifth by twelve days. It was not a change that the good peasantry could easily comprehend: but a test of the rightness of the innovation lay at hand. When would the thorn-bush bloom— on Christmas, Old Style, or Christmas, New Style? On the date of the new Christmas, they turned out with lanterns and candles to watch—and the thorn failed to bloom. Therefore it was not Christmas. They refused to go to church and pretend that it was. They waited until Christmas, Old Style, to finish their scientific experiment . . . and lo! the thorn blossomed. Therefore the Old Style calendar was right.

The Christmas tree bears flowers and fruits because of the blossoming trees and bushes of the first Noel. At least as far back as the sixteenth century, some southern Germans cut cherry and hawthorn boughs on Saint Andrew's Day (November thirtieth) and placed them in a pot of water in a warm room. By Christmas they spread and put forth full bloom. If the flowers were many, the new year would be goodly; if they did not prosper, neither would the coming year.

The Tree Stands

The forest ordinance from Ammerschweier, already cited, indicates that by the middle of the sixteenth century some Alsatians had passed from hanging greens to a standing tree. In other countries—eastern Germany, England, Holland, Switzerland,

Scandinavia, and Russia —the people constructed something out of greenery, which has been called a "pyramid." Here is one set of instructions for making it: From the four corners of a wooden base, erect some uprights of very moderate length, tapering them in together at the top. Use this frame on which to tie greenery of boxwood, fir, or pine, colored papers, and other decorations. Add candles. Top with a tinsel pennant. If you wish to indulge your fancy, landscape the base with a miniature garden.

Our lighted and garnished Christmas tree apparently came into being when the decorated Alsatian fir tree, moving eastward and northward, at last met the lighted pyramid somewhere in Germany. Even after this happened (we do not know when it took place) all the older forms—pyramid, holly decorated with an apple, hanging trees, and others—continued on; the pyramid, as late as 1917.

There is a charming story of how the Christmas tree was used in Wittenberg as far back as 1737. On Christmas Eve, the lady of the manor set up as many little fir trees as there were people for whom she had gifts. She stood the trees in a row according to size, and dressed them richly or slightly, in order of size. She placed gifts under each, lighted candles on them, and summoned the household. The largest and best-filled trees went to those she loved best. Finally came the servants, and to each went a humbler tree and gift.

By the later eighteenth century, the Christmas tree, now fully ornamented and benignly alight, had wandered far and wide through the hamlets and towns of Germany. In 1815, a princess of Nassau-Weilburg lighted a tree at the court of Vienna and urged Kaiser Franz I to adopt it. In the early nineteenth century it even crossed the eastern frontier into Poland; although the Poles have never taken it to their hearts as the Germans have. From Vienna, the tree journeyed to Prague, and today we find it in Britain, Scandinavia, the Lowlands, and France.

When was the tree first set up in America? We really do not know.

There are some tales about it: For instance, that the Hessian soldiers whom King George III sent over during our Revolutionary War celebrated Christmas in the way of their homeland while George Washington and his Continentals were wintering at Valley Forge. It is said, furthermore, that a farmer in the Catskills, named Mark Carr, in 1851 first sold Christmas trees in New York City. This suggests that by then at least part of the United States was so used to them that a farmer could make a profit by selling them to city people.

THE CHRIST CHILD'S TREE

WHEN A BABY BROTHER or sister arrives in a German family, there must be a present for the older child, called a "child's-foot." At least from the fourteenth century onward, the Christ Child has been a little brother to all small persons. At his birth, therefore, every boy and girl must receive a "child's-foot;" and so the gifts of Christmas are regarded. The tree, too, is his gift, and is called "Christ's tree."

Although the common folk who have created the Christmas tree are largely unfamiliar with its factual history, in their poetry they are more eloquent of its meaning than any chronicle can be. One Christmas Eve, long ago, says one of their legends, the dark wind and the white snow howled and drove about a forester's cottage, deep in the midst of tall trees. Inside, the forester and his family were warm and snug and thankful when a tiny knock came on the door. Startled, the forester arose quickly and opened it. There stood a small child, cold, exhausted, hungry. Quickly they took him in and shut out the storm. They warmed him by the fire, and fed him their goodly, plain food, and put him in their coziest bed.

The morning broke in a dazzling white such as they had never seen before. The angel choir had returned, with its great music that reaches down to shepherds and cottagers.

The Child stood before them, radiant now. He said, "There is nothing I can give you beyond what you already have, except one thing." From a fir tree he broke off a branch and planted it by the door. Straightway it blossomed. "Behold," he said, "my gift to you. Henceforth it shall always bear its fruits at Christmas, when all the world is empty and dead. To you it shall be a sign of faith that does not die."

EPILOGUE

A SCHOLAR HAS SAID that much or even most of the history of the Northland is contained in the two words *Yule* and *Christmas,* and in our telling, we have stressed the tale as it has developed in the Northland. The bias has no more back of it than the shape that the general history of our own country has taken since its founding.

Christmas, we have seen, is of the Mediterranean; and yet it could never be said of that world, as it can be of the Northland, that its history is contained in this festival. For the Mediterranean world already had not merely centuries, but millennia behind it, when Christ was born; and even the religion that he founded had traveled several centuries before it discovered its need of Christmas.

The Northland, on the other hand, was then only a child. Under the schooling that the Southland gave it in the last fifteen hundred years, it has grown to adulthood. The Northland began its growth under the guidance of the Christianity which had already learned the need of Christmas.

Thereupon, in the Middle Ages, Rome and the Northland together set forth on an adventure. It was new, and so colossal that we can call it nothing less than an adventure in art. It took on many forms of expression, which ranged over the entire realm of human affairs; it built a new world and molded a new kind of person. The inventions of the Gothic cathedral and the pipe organ are parts of this adventure. They are but examples of it in their own fields. They are, indeed, symbols of it. And so is Christmas; so much so, that each is hardly understandable without the other.

Christmas is a spontaneous drama of the common folk, a prayer, a hymn. All the while that Raphael was painting the Sistine Madonna, Frenchmen building the cathedral of Chartres, English bishops composing the *Book of Common Prayer*, Handel his *Messiah*, Bach his *B-Minor Mass*, the common people, out of whom these geniuses sprang, were composing Christmas.

The lifeblood of a people is its traditions, and Christmas has become great because men and women have given to it their deepest and most enduring selves. What they achieve in common, and what their common frustrations are, make of them one people. Then has the adventure of which Christmas, after all, is but a part, now closed?

Could we, at Christmas, stand away from Europe and the countries that have sprung from her across the seas, we should behold all of them doing the same thing, yet each in a way that is also somewhat peculiar to itself. These nations are not all of one birth; to some, birth has come sooner than to others. And when our fingers touch their Christmas, we are feeling their flesh and bone. Perhaps we shall best understand this if we particularly look at some of the poorer nations of the world and listen for their sounds. To their people at least, the notion of secular as distinct from religious life is an unreal thing. Religion is to many poor people not a garment, which they don on Sunday when they have cast workaday dress aside. It is something that walks the furrows and sits in the kitchen. It is the Angelus in the field, the saying of Grace. It is not just a solace; it is an aspiration.

Were you on Christmas Eve a guest in a poor home in Poland, you would eat from a table covered with a linen cloth, beneath which hay or straw has been laid. It is an old and pagan Slavic custom of the season, done over by these Christians to mean the bedding of the manger. Supper is not eaten before the head of the household has broken a consecrated wafer and shared it with every one present, in token that he is ready to share with all of them his last morsel.

A painting by Malczewski depicts a group of Polish exiles gathered about their manger-table to eat together the wafers sent from the homes they expect never to see again. A cloth covers the straw, a candle is on the table, a samovar for tea at the farther end, and part of a loaf of bread. We look at their faces: They are not ordinary; they are the kind whose destiny frequently is exile. To the common table each man has brought his sacred and unassailable inner solitude. The head of one is bowed in the shadow behind his uptilted soup-plate; another is holding his soup-plate forth to receive his wafer. The leader is standing; from a wrapper he is shaking into his palm

the wafers that have arrived from the homeland. Christmas is an intimate occasion, a family affair; and these men are the gathered fragments broken from so many families far away; families that have shared a common custom for generations. But there is here much more than separation from family and personal friends; these are children who are being denied the nourishment of their motherland at the very moment when, in street, in house and tavern and church, all of her life is welling up to meet the agony of the ages and the hope that yearly is reborn, this night, in the dead of winter.

So the music of the Chirstmas morning has its dark strain. It has always been there. The common folk of the Middle Ages, and those who are their descendants, in the simple wisdom sprung from their lives, have never shrunk from the note of sadness, of coming tragedy for which this birthday is a preparation. Sometimes it sounds in their carols; yet we hear no discord; only a sweeter and finer and deeper music.

While, then, we have stressed the Christmas of the Northland, we have remembered that this drama is greater even than what the Northland has given to it. To a wider range of lands and peoples, as well as to a longer span of time than the recent centuries, it has been a great confession: of failure, of frustration, yet of a faith and hope that for generations have answered death with a song of triumph. It is a wager placed on the side of the angels. Humankind has a long journey behind it, and a rugged journey thus far; nevertheless, in long perspective, a journey upward. And so it is that, in this our own short time, whatever be the challenge of despair, there live today those who are thinking more lofty and daring thoughts than ever before.

INDEX

ILLUSTRATIONS

❧

Other Seastone Titles

WHAT WOULD BUDDHA DO?: 101 Answers to Life's Daily Dilemmas
Franz Metcalf

Much as the "WWJD?" books help Christians live better lives by drawing on the wisdom of Jesus, this "WWBD?" book provides advice on improving your life by following the wisdom of another great teacher—Buddha. *Hardcover. $15.00*

THE SACRED EAST: An Illustrated Guide to Buddhism, Hinduism, Confucianism, Taoism and Shinto
C. Scott Littleton, General Editor

The Sacred East illuminates the main philosophies and religions of Asia, exploring the Hindu traditions of India, the richly varied Buddhist faith, the Confucian and Taoist beliefs of China and the Shinto religion of Japan. *Trade paper. $17.95*

JESUS AND BUDDHA: The Parallel Sayings
Marcus Borg, Editor   Introduction by Jack Kornfield

Traces the life stories and beliefs of Jesus and Buddha, then presents a comprehensive collection of their remarkably similar teachings on facing pages. *Trade paper. $14.00*

JESUS AND LAO TZU: The Parallel Sayings
Martin Aronson

Comparing the New Testament with the Tao Te Ching, Taoism's most sacred book, *Jesus and Lao Tzu: The Parallel Sayings* features an astonishing series of examples in which these two spiritual masters lead their followers down the same path in spite of differences in time and geography. *Hardcover. $19.00*

MUSIC OF SILENCE
David Steindl-Rast with Sharon Lebell   Introduction by Kathleen Norris

A noted Benedictine monk shows us how to incorporate the sacred meaning of monastic life into our everyday world by paying attention to the "seasons of the day" and the enlivening messages to be found in each moment. *Trade paper. $12.00*

BEFORE HE WAS BUDDHA: The Life of Siddhartha
Hammalawa Saddhatissa   Introduction by Jack Kornfield

Written in a lucid, flowing style, this biographical profile reveals the strength and gentleness of Buddha's character and brings to life the compassion that gave his teachings universal appeal. *Trade paper. $12.00*

THE GOSPEL OF THOMAS: Unearthing the Lost Words of Jesus
John Dart and Ray Riegert   Introduction by John Dominic Crossan

Details the discovery of the greatest collection of apocryphal Christian documents ever found. The dramatic narrative history is combined with an annotated translation of The Gospel of Thomas. *Trade paper. $12.00*

DEAD SEA SCROLLS: The Complete Story
Dr. Jonathan Campbell

Dispels rumors surrounding the Scrolls and recounts the actual events of their unearthing, laying the groundwork for a vivid investigation of the relevance of the Scrolls to our times. *Trade paper. $12.95*

WHAT WOULD SHAKESPEARE DO?: Personal Advice from the Bard
Jess Winfield

In a friendly, straightforward fashion, *What Would Shakespeare Do?* uncovers for us all the personal advice contained in the Bard's immortal words. *WWSD?* explores ideas that still resonate today: sex and love, youth and aging, morals and the meaning of life. *Hardcover. $16.00*

To order these titles or other Seastone books call 800-377-2542 or 510-601-8301, e-mail ulysses@ulyssespress.com or write to Ulysses Press, P.O. Box 3440, Berkeley, CA 94703. There is no charge for shipping on retail orders. California residents must include sales tax. Allow two to three weeks for delivery

ABOUT THE AUTHORS

After a reknowned career as an author, anthropologist and Episcopalian priest, DR. EARL W. COUNT recently died at age 97. During his life he served as department chairman and professor emeritus at Hamilton College (NY) and was profiled in the *New York Times*.

His widow ALICE LAWSON COUNT, a published musician, retired harpist and historical musicologist, has updated her husband's original work for this edition.

DAN WAKEFIELD is the author of *Expect a Miracle* and *Creating from the Spirit*. He also wrote the script of the movie "Going All The Way," based on his best-selling novel.